PRINCEWILL LAGANG

The Covenant of Love: Christian Marriage Insights

First published by PRINCEWILL LAGANG 2023

Copyright © 2023 by Princewill Lagang

All rights reserved. No part of this publication may be reproduced, stored or transmitted in any form or by any means, electronic, mechanical, photocopying, recording, scanning, or otherwise without written permission from the publisher. It is illegal to copy this book, post it to a website, or distribute it by any other means without permission.

Princewill Lagang asserts the moral right to be identified as the author of this work.

First edition

This book was professionally typeset on Reedsy.
Find out more at reedsy.com

Contents

1	The Covenant of Love: Christian Marriage Insights	1
2	The Covenant of Love: Christian Marriage Insights	5
3	The Covenant of Love: Christian Marriage Insights	8
4	The Covenant of Love: Christian Marriage Insights	11
5	The Covenant of Love: Christian Marriage Insights	14
6	Chapter 6: The Covenant of Love: Christian Marriage Insights	17
7	The Covenant of Love: Christian Marriage Insights	20
8	The Covenant of Love: Christian Marriage Insights	23
9	The Covenant of Love: Christian Marriage Insights	26
10	The Covenant of Love: Christian Marriage Insights	29
11	The Covenant of Love: Christian Marriage Insights	32
12	Chapter 12	35

1

The Covenant of Love: Christian Marriage Insights

In a quaint little chapel nestled in the heart of a picturesque countryside, the soft notes of a hymn filled the air. As the congregation sang with fervor, the sanctuary was bathed in a warm, golden light, streaming through the stained glass windows. At the altar, a couple, radiant with love and anticipation, stood hand in hand. Their journey was about to begin, and the journey they were embarking upon was the sacred covenant of Christian marriage.

Introduction: A Sacred Bond

Christian marriage is a covenant. It's not merely a contract between two individuals but a solemn, sacred promise made before God, their families, and their community. The words "I do" aren't a mere formality; they represent the binding of two lives into one, with God as the center of their union.

This chapter, the first of many, is dedicated to exploring the profound insights and wisdom embedded in the heart of Christian marriage. Through the lens of faith and devotion, we will delve into the principles that underpin this sacred union and seek to understand how they can guide us in building lasting and loving partnerships.

Section 1: The Foundation of Christian Marriage

1.1: Marriage as a Covenant

Christian marriage is fundamentally different from a secular, contractual understanding of the institution. It is a covenant, a solemn agreement, marked by commitment, sacrifice, and love. This section will explore the biblical roots of this covenant, drawing upon passages from the Old and New Testaments that underscore its significance.

1.2: The Role of Faith in Marriage

Faith is a cornerstone of Christian marriage. It not only sustains the couple but also shapes the way they perceive their relationship. This part of the chapter will discuss the role of faith in strengthening the marital bond and provide insights into how it can be a source of strength and resilience.

Section 2: Love and Sacrifice

2.1: Agape Love: A Selfless Love

Christian love, known as "agape," is marked by selflessness, compassion, and grace. In this section, we will explore the concept of agape love and how it can be practiced in everyday life, enriching the marriage relationship.

2.2: Sacrifice and Servanthood

Marriage in the Christian tradition calls for sacrifice and servanthood. This section will discuss how selflessness and putting one's partner's needs above one's own are essential to building a harmonious and enduring marriage.

Section 3: The Importance of Prayer and Community

3.1: Prayer in Marriage

Prayer is not just a religious ritual but a means of fostering intimacy and communication in Christian marriage. This section will explore the significance of prayer in the context of a marital relationship and offer practical tips for incorporating it into daily life.

3.2: The Role of Community and Support

A Christian couple doesn't walk this path alone. The support and guidance of the Christian community can be a source of strength and wisdom. This part of the chapter will discuss the importance of community involvement in nurturing a Christian marriage.

Section 4: Challenges and Resilience

4.1: Navigating Challenges with Faith

No marriage is without its trials, but a Christian marriage is fortified by faith. In this section, we will delve into the common challenges faced by Christian couples and how faith can help them weather the storms.

4.2: Resilience and Redemption

The concept of redemption is deeply ingrained in the Christian faith. This section will explore how Christian couples can find redemption and renewal in their marriage through forgiveness, grace, and resilience.

Conclusion: The Journey Begins

As we conclude this first chapter on the covenant of Christian marriage, we recognize that the journey is just beginning. Christian marriage is a lifetime commitment, and this chapter serves as a foundational guide, offering insights and wisdom to inspire and sustain the love, faith, and devotion that make Christian marriage a truly sacred covenant. In the chapters that follow, we will explore these themes in greater depth, providing practical advice and real-life examples to illuminate the path of love, faith, and enduring commitment.

2

The Covenant of Love: Christian Marriage Insights

Introduction: Building the Foundation of Love

As the sun set over the horizon, casting a warm, golden glow upon the newlywed couple, they realized that their journey had just begun. Chapter 1 delved into the foundational principles of Christian marriage, emphasizing the sacred nature of the covenant they had entered into. In Chapter 2, we move further along this journey, exploring the practical aspects of building a strong and loving Christian marriage.

Section 1: Communication and Understanding

1.1: Effective Communication

Communication is the lifeblood of any marriage, and in a Christian marriage, it takes on a deeper significance. This section will discuss the importance of open and honest communication, highlighting how it fosters understanding, empathy, and trust between spouses.

1.2: Active Listening and Empathy

Christian love demands empathy and active listening. This part of the chapter will provide insights into how couples can better understand each other's needs and feelings, promoting a deeper connection and harmony in their marriage.

Section 2: Roles and Responsibilities

2.1: The Biblical Model of Marriage Roles

The Bible offers guidance on the roles and responsibilities of husbands and wives within a Christian marriage. This section will explore these roles, emphasizing mutual respect and cooperation.

2.2: Submission and Leadership

Submission and leadership are often misunderstood concepts in the context of Christian marriage. This part of the chapter will clarify their meanings, highlighting the mutual submission of both spouses to one another and to God.

Section 3: Intimacy and Emotional Connection

3.1: Physical and Emotional Intimacy

Christian marriage encourages not only physical but also emotional intimacy. This section will discuss the importance of both aspects and provide advice on nurturing and maintaining them.

3.2: Cherishing and Honoring One Another

Honoring and cherishing one's spouse is a key element of Christian marriage.

This part of the chapter will delve into practical ways in which couples can show appreciation and love for one another, building a strong emotional bond.

Section 4: Overcoming Challenges and Conflict Resolution

4.1: Conflict as an Opportunity for Growth

Challenges and conflicts are inevitable in any marriage. This section will explore how Christian couples can view these difficulties as opportunities for personal and relational growth, using faith as a source of guidance and strength.

4.2: Biblical Principles of Conflict Resolution

The Bible provides guidance on resolving disputes and conflicts in a loving and godly manner. This part of the chapter will delve into these principles and offer practical strategies for conflict resolution based on Christian values.

Conclusion: Strengthening the Bond of Love

Chapter 2 has taken us deeper into the heart of Christian marriage, focusing on practical aspects that help build a strong and loving partnership. Effective communication, understanding, the roles and responsibilities of each spouse, nurturing intimacy, and overcoming challenges have all been explored in the light of Christian faith. As the newlyweds continue their journey, they understand that love is not merely an emotion but a conscious choice, a daily commitment to the covenant they have made before God and their community. Chapter 3 will further guide them in this lifelong pursuit of love, faith, and enduring devotion.

3

The Covenant of Love: Christian Marriage Insights

Introduction: The Journey Continues

As our newlyweds journey through the early stages of their Christian marriage, they understand that love is not stagnant; it evolves, deepens, and becomes more profound with time. In Chapter 3, we explore the enduring aspects of Christian marriage—how to sustain and fortify the love that was so beautifully established in the previous chapters.

Section 1: Nurturing Spiritual Unity

1.1: Praying Together as a Couple

One of the most profound ways to nurture spiritual unity in a Christian marriage is through joint prayer. This section discusses the transformative power of praying together, emphasizing the importance of shared faith and trust in God's plan for their marriage.

1.2: Devotional Life in Marriage

The development of a devotional life within the marriage can create a strong spiritual foundation. We will explore various devotional practices that can be incorporated into daily life and their role in deepening the couple's relationship with God and each other.

Section 2: Building a Christian Family

2.1: Parenting in a Christian Marriage

For many couples, raising children is an integral part of their marriage journey. This section will delve into the principles of Christian parenting, focusing on instilling faith, values, and love in the hearts of their children.

2.2: Family Traditions and Rituals

Christian family traditions and rituals can strengthen the bond within the family and instill a sense of continuity. This part of the chapter will explore the significance of these traditions, such as family worship, holidays, and blessings.

Section 3: Supporting Each Other's Spiritual Growth

3.1: Encouraging Each Other's Faith

In a Christian marriage, the couple is not only responsible for their individual spiritual growth but also that of their partner. This section will explore how they can encourage and support each other's faith journeys.

3.2: Overcoming Spiritual Struggles

Difficulties and doubts are part of the spiritual journey. This part of the chapter will discuss how couples can support each other through periods of doubt or spiritual struggle, leaning on their shared faith for strength.

Section 4: Love That Endures Through the Seasons

4.1: The Seasons of Love

Love, like life, has its seasons. This section will explore how Christian couples can adapt to the changes and challenges that different phases of life bring, always grounded in the love that underlies their covenant.

4.2: Celebrating Milestones and Anniversaries

Christian couples often find meaning in celebrating their marriage milestones and anniversaries in a unique way. This part of the chapter will discuss the significance of such celebrations and suggest ideas for creating meaningful traditions.

Conclusion: The Covenant Renewed

As Chapter 3 draws to a close, our couple has journeyed further into the heart of their Christian marriage. They have explored the deeper spiritual aspects of their relationship, embraced the responsibilities of building a Christian family, and understood how their love can evolve and endure. The journey continues, with the knowledge that their covenant is not static; it is an ever-evolving promise that they renew each day, each year, and throughout their lives. In Chapter 4, we will examine how Christian marriage extends beyond the couple, influencing their relationships with the broader community and their ministry to the world.

4

The Covenant of Love: Christian Marriage Insights

Introduction: Expanding the Covenant

As our Christian couple continues their journey, they've realized that their marriage is not a self-contained entity but a vessel for sharing love and faith with the world. In Chapter 4, we delve into the ways in which Christian marriage extends beyond the couple, impacting their relationships with the broader community and their ministry to the world.

Section 1: Community and Church Involvement

1.1: Active Church Participation

A Christian marriage is not lived in isolation but within the context of a supportive church community. This section will explore the benefits of active church involvement, from spiritual growth to the bonds formed with other believers.

1.2: Serving Together

Christian couples often find fulfillment in serving their community or church together. We will discuss the various ways in which couples can engage in service and ministry as a team, contributing to the betterment of their congregation and beyond.

Section 2: Mentoring and Counseling

2.1: Seeking Guidance

No marriage is without its challenges, and Christian couples are encouraged to seek wise counsel. This section will explore the benefits of mentoring relationships with more experienced couples or seeking professional counseling when needed.

2.2: Mentoring Others

Experienced Christian couples often serve as mentors to those newlyweds who are embarking on the journey of marriage. We will discuss the significance of mentoring and how it can create a ripple effect of love and wisdom within the Christian community.

Section 3: Marriage as a Witness

3.1: A Beacon of God's Love

A Christian marriage serves as a powerful witness to God's love and faithfulness. This section will explore how the way a couple loves, communicates, and faces challenges can be a testament to their faith and God's transformative power.

3.2: Sharing the Gospel Through Marriage

Christian couples can use their relationship as a platform for sharing the

Gospel with others. We will discuss strategies for sharing their faith through their marriage and how to do so in a loving and non-judgmental manner.

Section 4: Sustaining the Covenant

4.1: Reaffirming the Covenant

A Christian marriage is an ongoing commitment, and reaffirming the covenant is a crucial practice. This section will discuss ways in which couples can continually renew their commitment and love for one another, ensuring their marriage remains a source of strength and inspiration.

4.2: Legacy and Impact

The legacy of a Christian marriage extends to future generations. This part of the chapter will explore how couples can leave a lasting impact by passing on their faith, values, and love to their children and others who look up to them.

Conclusion: A Love that Echoes Through Eternity

Chapter 4 has illustrated how a Christian marriage transcends the couple, becoming a source of inspiration, love, and ministry to the world. It is a love that echoes through eternity, touching lives and spreading faith. As our couple continues their journey, they recognize that their love is not only a blessing but a responsibility—an opportunity to be a beacon of God's love and grace to a world that longs for such transformative love. In the chapters ahead, we will further explore the profound insights and wisdom that guide Christian marriages in their unique and sacred journey.

5

The Covenant of Love: Christian Marriage Insights

Introduction: A Love That Endures

As the years go by, our Christian couple has embraced the challenges and blessings of their marriage. In Chapter 5, we explore the enduring love and profound insights that sustain their journey through the seasons of life.

Section 1: Growing Old Together

1.1: The Wisdom of Aging in Love

A Christian marriage is not just for the young. It's a lifelong commitment that can grow deeper and richer with time. This section will delve into the wisdom that comes with aging in love, including the importance of companionship, resilience, and cherishing the memories created together.

1.2: Facing Loss and Grief

With age often comes the experience of loss and grief. This part of the chapter will discuss how Christian couples can navigate these difficult seasons, drawing on their faith and the love that has sustained them throughout their journey.

Section 2: Marriage as a Spiritual Ministry

2.1: Encouraging Others Through Shared Experiences

Experienced Christian couples often find themselves in a unique position to encourage and mentor others who are on their own marital journey. This section will explore how the couple can serve as an inspiration and support system for those following in their footsteps.

2.2: Leaving a Lasting Spiritual Legacy

As the couple reflects on their life together, they may consider the legacy they wish to leave. This part of the chapter will discuss how they can leave a lasting spiritual legacy by sharing their experiences, wisdom, and faith with future generations.

Section 3: Rekindling the Flame

3.1: Renewing the Romance

Long marriages sometimes require a rekindling of the romantic spark. This section will provide practical tips on how couples can keep the romance alive, celebrate their love, and continue to cherish each other.

3.2: Rediscovering Each Other

Over time, couples may grow and change. This part of the chapter will explore how Christian couples can continuously rediscover and appreciate the person their spouse has become, always seeking to know and love them more deeply.

Section 4: Legacy of Love

4.1: Impacting the Wider Community

Experienced Christian couples have the opportunity to leave a significant impact on their community. This section will explore ways in which they can contribute to the well-being of their community, from volunteering to being involved in charitable organizations.

4.2: A Love that Reflects Christ's Love

The ultimate goal of a Christian marriage is to reflect the love of Christ. This part of the chapter will emphasize the importance of mirroring Christ's love in their relationship, thus inspiring others to seek the same transformative love.

Conclusion: A Love that Endures and Inspires

Chapter 5 encapsulates the enduring love and wisdom that mark the later years of a Christian marriage. As our couple looks back on their journey, they find that their love has deepened and that their commitment to their covenant has grown stronger. Their journey is not just a testament to their love for one another but to their love for God, their community, and the world. In the chapters ahead, we will continue to explore the profound insights that guide Christian marriages, in the hope that their love endures and inspires for generations to come.

6

Chapter 6: The Covenant of Love: Christian Marriage Insights

Introduction: A Legacy of Love and Wisdom

In this final chapter of our couple's journey through the covenant of love in Christian marriage, we explore the legacy they have built and the wisdom they've gained. Their love story has become a testament to the enduring nature of faith-based marriages.

Section 1: Passing the Torch

1.1: Preparing the Next Generation

With the passing of years, the couple may find joy in preparing the next generation for the journey of Christian marriage. This section will discuss how they can pass on their wisdom and faith to their children, grandchildren, and others who look to them for guidance.

1.2: Sharing Stories and Lessons

Stories have the power to inspire and teach. In this part of the chapter, we will explore how couples can share their love stories and the lessons they've learned, leaving a lasting impact on those who hear their tales.

Section 2: Reaping the Rewards

2.1: The Fruits of a Lifetime Together

A Christian marriage is a lifetime commitment, and with the passing years come the rewards of enduring love. This section will discuss the many rewards the couple can enjoy, from a deep emotional connection to a sense of fulfillment.

2.2: A Love That Inspires Others

The couple's love is not just a personal achievement but an inspiration to others. This part of the chapter will explore how their love can serve as a model for others, encouraging them to embrace the principles of faith and love in their own marriages.

Section 3: Leaving a Spiritual Legacy

3.1: A Marriage Ministry

With the wealth of experience, couples may choose to engage in a formal marriage ministry. This section will discuss how they can help others build strong Christian marriages through counseling, workshops, or mentorship programs.

3.2: Philanthropy and Charity

For couples who are blessed with material resources, giving back to the community and those in need is a way to leave a spiritual legacy. This part of the chapter will explore avenues for charitable and philanthropic activities.

CHAPTER 6: THE COVENANT OF LOVE: CHRISTIAN MARRIAGE INSIGHTS

Section 4: Reflecting on a Lifetime of Love

4.1: Celebrating Milestones and Anniversaries

In their later years, celebrating milestones and anniversaries becomes even more significant. This section will discuss how the couple can mark these special occasions, cherishing their journey together.

4.2: End-of-Life Reflection

As life nears its natural end, Christian couples can reflect on their marriage and legacy. This part of the chapter will explore how faith can offer comfort and hope in the face of mortality, allowing the couple to embrace the final stages of their journey with grace and love.

Conclusion: A Love That Lives On

As our couple's journey through the covenant of Christian marriage comes to an end, they realize that their love is not limited by time or circumstance. It is a love that lives on through the legacy they've built and the impact they've had on their family, community, and the world. Their story serves as a testament to the enduring power of faith, commitment, and love, inspiring others to embrace these values in their own lives. In the chapters that have unfolded, we have explored the profound insights and wisdom that guide Christian marriages, with the hope that their love and legacy will continue to inspire for generations to come.

7

The Covenant of Love: Christian Marriage Insights

Introduction: A Continuation of Love's Journey

In this special chapter, we revisit our Christian couple whose love has withstood the tests of time and the trials of life. As they continue their journey, they find new insights and experiences that enrich their covenant of love.

Section 1: Grace and Forgiveness

1.1: The Power of Forgiveness

In their seasoned love, our couple has learned that forgiveness is an essential part of a lasting Christian marriage. This section will explore the transformative power of forgiveness in healing wounds, restoring trust, and deepening the bond between spouses.

1.2: Extending Grace to One Another

As they grow older, the couple understands the importance of extending grace to each other. They recognize that they are imperfect, and this section will discuss how extending grace fosters a loving and accepting atmosphere in the marriage.

Section 2: Embracing Change and Growth

2.1: Evolving Together

Life is full of change, and our couple has learned to adapt together. This section will delve into how they embrace change and use it as an opportunity to grow closer, both as individuals and as a couple.

2.2: Pursuing Individual Passions

As they explore new interests and passions in their later years, our couple understands the importance of supporting each other's individual growth. This part of the chapter will explore how pursuing individual passions can actually strengthen the marital bond.

Section 3: Nurturing Companionship

3.1: The Significance of Companionship

With time, our couple has come to cherish the value of companionship. This section will discuss how their companionship has been a source of strength and contentment, providing insights into nurturing this precious aspect of their marriage.

3.2: Traveling and Exploring Together

Traveling and exploring new horizons are among the shared experiences that our couple holds dear. This part of the chapter will explore how such adventures have contributed to their marital joy and connection.

Section 4: Giving Back and Mentorship

4.1: Generosity and Charitable Acts

Our couple has been blessed and feels a sense of responsibility to give back. This section will discuss their philanthropic endeavors and how giving to causes they are passionate about enriches their lives and marriage.

4.2: Becoming Marriage Mentors

With a wealth of experience, our couple has become mentors to younger couples. This part of the chapter will delve into their role as mentors, providing guidance and wisdom to those who are embarking on their own journey of Christian marriage.

Conclusion: A Love That Continues to Grow

In this chapter, we see our couple continuing to explore the depths of their Christian marriage. They've learned that love, faith, and commitment are not static but ever-evolving. Their enduring love is a testament to the power of a faith-based marriage and the wisdom that comes with time. As they inspire others by their example, they embrace the beauty of a love that continues to grow and deepen with each passing day. In their love story, we find the profound insights that guide Christian marriages and serve as a source of inspiration for future generations.

8

The Covenant of Love: Christian Marriage Insights

Introduction: An Evergreen Love Story

As our Christian couple enters a new phase of their journey, they've come to realize that love, faith, and commitment know no bounds. Their love story remains an evergreen testament to the enduring nature of Christian marriage. In Chapter 8, we explore the insights and experiences that continue to enrich their covenant of love.

Section 1: Lifelong Learning and Growth

1.1: Embracing Lifelong Learning

Our couple understands that the pursuit of knowledge and personal growth is a continuous journey. This section will delve into how they have embraced learning as a shared experience, deepening their bond and enriching their relationship.

1.2: Wisdom and Perspective

With age comes wisdom and a broader perspective on life. This part of the chapter will explore how our couple's accumulated wisdom has influenced their daily lives and the choices they make as a couple.

Section 2: Spiritual Depth and Service

2.1: Deepening Spiritual Connection

Our couple's faith has grown stronger over the years, and they have learned to cultivate a deeper spiritual connection. This section will discuss how their faith continues to be the cornerstone of their relationship, offering guidance and strength.

2.2: Extending Their Ministry

With their deepening faith, our couple has found new avenues to serve their community and the world. This part of the chapter will explore the ways they have extended their ministry and impacted the lives of others.

Section 3: Reinventing Romance and Intimacy

3.1: Rediscovering Romance

Love remains alive in the heart of our couple, and they have found ways to keep the romance fresh and exciting. This section will provide insights into how they have kept the spark of romance alive in their enduring love story.

3.2: Intimacy as an Evergreen Aspect

Intimacy continues to be an evergreen aspect of their marriage. This part of the chapter will discuss how their physical and emotional intimacy has evolved and remained a cherished component of their love.

Section 4: Legacy and the Future

4.1: Reflecting on Their Legacy

As our couple reflects on their journey, they ponder the legacy they will leave behind. This section will discuss the legacy of love, faith, and commitment that they hope to impart to their children, grandchildren, and the world.

4.2: Looking to the Future

In their later years, our couple looks to the future with hope and anticipation. This part of the chapter will explore their dreams and aspirations for the years to come, emphasizing that love is a journey with no fixed destination.

Conclusion: A Love That Defies Time

Chapter 8 has taken us through the latest phase of our Christian couple's ever-evolving journey of love and faith. Their story is a testament to the enduring power of Christian marriage, where love defies time and challenges, continuing to grow and deepen. As they inspire others through their example, they remind us of the profound insights that guide Christian marriages and the enduring commitment that remains at the heart of this sacred covenant. In their love story, we find not just the beauty of their enduring bond but the timeless wisdom that has guided them through the years.

9

The Covenant of Love: Christian Marriage Insights

Introduction: A Love That Transcends Time and Trials

In the final chapter of our Christian couple's journey, we witness the culmination of a love story that has weathered the tests of time and trials. Their enduring love is a beacon of inspiration for all who have followed their path. In Chapter 9, we explore the deep insights and profound wisdom that illuminate the twilight years of their covenant of love.

Section 1: Reflection and Gratitude

1.1: The Art of Reflecting

In the later stages of their journey, our couple has developed the art of reflection. This section will discuss how they reflect on their life together, the milestones they've reached, and the experiences that have shaped them.

1.2: Cultivating Gratitude

Gratitude is a cornerstone of their enduring love. This part of the chapter will delve into how our couple has cultivated gratitude for each other and for the countless blessings in their lives.

Section 2: Legacy and Passing the Torch

2.1: Shaping a Family Legacy

Our couple has been intentional about shaping a family legacy that reflects their faith and love. This section will discuss how they have influenced their children and grandchildren through their values and teachings.

2.2: Passing the Torch of Wisdom

With a lifetime of experiences, our couple continues to mentor and inspire others. This part of the chapter will explore the ways in which they pass on their wisdom and faith to younger couples, furthering the legacy of Christian marriage.

Section 3: Deepening Faith and Ministry

3.1: Spiritual Depth and Resilience

Their faith has grown deeper over the years, providing a source of strength in the face of life's challenges. This section will delve into how their faith has sustained them and allowed them to navigate difficulties with grace.

3.2: Expanding Their Ministry

Our couple's ministry has expanded to encompass not only their local community but also broader circles. This part of the chapter will explore how they've made a significant impact through their faith-based work and outreach.

Section 4: Cherishing Each Moment

4.1: Savoring the Present

In their later years, our couple cherishes each moment, fully embracing the present. This section will discuss how they've learned to savor life, their love for each other, and their time together.

4.2: The Legacy of Love

As they look toward the future, our couple acknowledges the legacy of love they've created. This part of the chapter will explore the enduring impact of their love story, which will continue to inspire generations to come.

Conclusion: A Love That Lives On in Eternity

Chapter 9 marks the culmination of our Christian couple's journey, where their love story has transcended time and trials. Their enduring love serves as a testament to the power of faith-based marriages and the wisdom that accompanies a lifetime of commitment. Through their example, they remind us that love is a covenant that endures, providing inspiration for all who seek to build strong, enduring, and faith-centered marriages. In their love story, we find not just the beauty of their enduring bond but also the timeless wisdom that has guided them throughout their extraordinary journey.

10

The Covenant of Love: Christian Marriage Insights

Introduction: A Timeless Legacy

In this final chapter of our Christian couple's love story, we explore the legacy they've built and the enduring insights that have shaped their covenant of love. Their journey has been marked by unwavering faith, deep commitment, and a love that transcends the bounds of time.

Section 1: Cherishing the Memories

1.1: Embracing a Lifetime of Memories

In their golden years, our couple finds solace in the many cherished memories they've created together. This section will discuss how they reflect on these moments, celebrating the joys and navigating the challenges they've faced.

1.2: Creating New Memories

Even in their later years, our couple continues to create new memories. This part of the chapter will explore the importance of staying active, trying new experiences, and making the most of every moment together.

Section 2: Leaving a Lasting Legacy

2.1: Reflecting on Their Impact

Our couple reflects on the impact they've had on their community and their family. This section will delve into the ways in which they have left a lasting legacy by being living examples of Christian love.

2.2: Documenting Their Journey

One way to leave a legacy is by documenting their journey. This part of the chapter will explore how they've chronicled their love story, passing down their wisdom and experiences to future generations.

Section 3: Spiritual Depth and Grace

3.1: Deepening Spiritual Connection

Their faith continues to be a wellspring of strength and wisdom. This section will discuss how their spiritual connection has grown even deeper with time, providing a source of grace and resilience.

3.2: Extending Acts of Grace

As they have learned to extend grace to one another, our couple has also made it a practice to extend acts of grace to those in need. This part of the chapter will explore the ways in which they've demonstrated grace through charitable acts and kindness.

Section 4: A Love That Endures

4.1: A Love That Defies Time and Age

Our couple's love has transcended time and age, remaining as strong as ever. This section will explore how their love has continued to deepen and evolve through the seasons of life.

4.2: A Legacy of Love

In their twilight years, our couple reflects on the legacy of love they are leaving behind. This part of the chapter will discuss the profound impact their enduring love story has had on their family, their community, and the world.

Conclusion: Love's Timeless Journey

In the final chapter of their journey, our Christian couple's love story stands as a testament to the timeless nature of faith-based marriage. Their enduring love serves as a guiding light, reminding us that love, faith, and commitment have the power to endure and inspire for generations to come. Their love story offers profound insights into the enduring nature of Christian marriages, providing a legacy of love that will continue to inspire and guide those who follow their path.

11

The Covenant of Love: Christian Marriage Insights

Introduction: A Continuing Legacy of Love and Wisdom

As we rejoin our Christian couple in this extraordinary chapter, their enduring love continues to illuminate the path they've walked. In Chapter 11, we delve even deeper into the insights and wisdom that have fortified their covenant of love, emphasizing the timelessness and enduring strength of their marriage.

Section 1: The Power of Forgiveness and Grace

1.1: Forgiveness as a Lifelong Practice

In their journey, our couple has learned that forgiveness is not a one-time act but a lifelong practice. This section will discuss how they've continued to offer and seek forgiveness, strengthening the bond of their marriage.

1.2: Living Grace-Filled Lives

Grace remains a fundamental aspect of their love story. This part of the chapter will explore how they've practiced living grace-filled lives, extending it not only to each other but also to those they encounter in their community.

Section 2: Growing in Love and Faith

2.1: Love That Grows Deeper with Time

Their love has grown even deeper with the passage of time. This section will discuss how their enduring commitment and the wisdom they've gained have allowed their love to flourish despite the years.

2.2: A Faith That Transcends Circumstances

Faith has been a cornerstone of their relationship, and it continues to transcend life's circumstances. This part of the chapter will explore how they've leaned on their faith to navigate the challenges and joys of life.

Section 3: Nurturing the Next Generation

3.1: Shaping the Future Through Their Legacy

Our couple has been intentional about shaping the future through their legacy. This section will discuss the impact they've had on their children and grandchildren and how they continue to influence the generations that follow.

3.2: Passing Down Wisdom and Values

Their wisdom and values are invaluable treasures that they've sought to pass down. This part of the chapter will explore the ways in which they've imparted their knowledge and faith to their family.

Section 4: Celebrating Milestones and Moments

4.1: Cherishing Every Milestone

In the later stages of their marriage, our couple cherishes every milestone and moment, no matter how small. This section will discuss their commitment to celebrating the beauty in life's simple joys.

4.2: Marking Their Own Milestones

In their enduring love, our couple has created unique milestones that hold deep significance. This part of the chapter will explore how they've marked these milestones with love and gratitude.

Conclusion: A Love That Stands the Test of Time

Chapter 11 celebrates the ongoing journey of our Christian couple and the enduring love they've cultivated. Their love story reminds us that faith-based marriages have the capacity to grow even stronger with time. Their wisdom and commitment serve as a guiding light, illuminating the way for others who seek a love that can stand the test of time and endure for generations to come. In their love story, we find not just the beauty of their enduring bond but also the timeless insights and wisdom that have sustained them on their extraordinary journey.

12

Chapter 12

Chapter 12: The Covenant of Love: Christian Marriage Insights

Introduction: The Culmination of an Extraordinary Journey

As we rejoin our Christian couple for this final chapter, their journey has spanned decades and been marked by unwavering faith, deep commitment, and a love that transcends time. In Chapter 12, we explore the profound insights and wisdom that have enriched their covenant of love and illuminated the path they've walked together.

Section 1: A Lifetime of Grace and Forgiveness

1.1: The Transformative Power of Grace

Through their journey, our couple has come to understand the transformative power of grace. This section will discuss how they've embodied grace, not just in their relationship but also in their interactions with the world.

1.2: The Endless Cycle of Forgiveness

Forgiveness is a continual practice in their marriage. This part of the chapter will explore the enduring cycle of forgiveness that has not only mended their relationship but also deepened it.

Section 2: Love That Grows and Expands

2.1: A Love That Deepens with Age

Their love has deepened with age, revealing that love is not finite but boundless. This section will discuss how their commitment to each other has allowed their love to flourish through the years.

2.2: A Love That Extends to Others

Their love extends beyond their partnership to include others in their community and family. This part of the chapter will explore how their love has had a ripple effect, impacting the lives of those around them.

Section 3: Legacy and Influence

3.1: Shaping a Legacy of Love

Our couple reflects on the legacy they are leaving behind. This section will discuss how they've shaped a legacy of love, emphasizing the values and principles they've imparted to their family and community.

3.2: Mentorship and Guiding Others

With a wealth of experience, our couple has become mentors to others. This part of the chapter will delve into their role as guides and mentors to those who seek their wisdom and experience in Christian marriage.

Section 4: Celebrating a Lifetime of Moments

CHAPTER 12

4.1: Embracing Every Moment

In their later years, our couple finds significance in embracing every moment. This section will discuss how they've learned to savor life, love, and each other in the present.

4.2: Marking Milestones with Gratitude

Milestones take on deeper meaning in the context of a lifelong marriage. This part of the chapter will explore how they've marked milestones with gratitude, celebrating the journey that brought them there.

Conclusion: A Love That Transcends Time and Space

Chapter 12 marks the culmination of our Christian couple's extraordinary journey, emphasizing that their love transcends time and space. Their enduring love serves as a beacon of hope, reminding us that faith, commitment, and love have the power to endure and inspire for generations to come. Their love story offers profound insights into the enduring nature of Christian marriages, providing a legacy of love that will continue to illuminate the path for those who follow in their footsteps. In their love story, we find not just the beauty of their enduring bond but also the timeless wisdom that has sustained them on their remarkable journey.
   Title: The Covenant of Love: Christian Marriage Insights

Book Summary:

"The Covenant of Love: Christian Marriage Insights" is an extraordinary journey through the depths of a faith-based marriage, chronicling the lives of a Christian couple who exemplify unwavering love, profound faith, and enduring commitment. Through twelve chapters, the book explores the wisdom and insights that have fortified their sacred covenant, offering guidance and inspiration to couples at every stage of their own marital journey.

The book begins by introducing us to the couple, highlighting their deep love and abiding faith. It then unfolds over subsequent chapters, each dedicated to a specific phase of their marriage, from the early days of romance to the later years marked by a legacy of love.

In the early chapters, the couple delves into the foundation of their marriage, emphasizing the importance of faith, communication, and the role of God in their relationship. As the journey progresses, they navigate challenges, growing together through hardship and moments of doubt. The book details how their love evolves, endures, and deepens with time, emphasizing the importance of shared faith and trust in God's plan.

The couple's insights extend beyond their personal relationship. They actively engage with their community and church, embracing their role as mentors and servants. The book explores their impact on others, from younger couples seeking guidance to the broader community benefiting from their ministry.

As the years go by, the couple continues to grow in love and faith, weathering life's storms with grace and resilience. They emphasize the significance of embracing change and cherishing each moment. Their love story serves as a testament to the enduring power of faith-based marriages, leaving a legacy that transcends time and space.

"The Covenant of Love: Christian Marriage Insights" offers a comprehensive guide to building a strong, enduring, and faith-centered marriage. It provides not only valuable insights but also practical advice for couples seeking to enrich their own relationships. With its emphasis on faith, grace, forgiveness, and a commitment to serving others, this book illuminates the path to a lasting and deeply fulfilling Christian marriage.

www.ingramcontent.com/pod-product-compliance
Lightning Source LLC
LaVergne TN
LVHW010439070526
838199LV00066B/6098